SCHIRMER'S LIBRARY
OF MUSICAL CLASSICS

Vol. 2041

SERGEY PROKOFIEV

Peter and the Wolf

Symphonic Tale for Children

For Piano

(English, French, and Spanish Texts)

Piano reduction by the composer

Boosey & Hawkes Music Publishers Ltd.
Sole Selling Agents of Anglo-Soviet Music Press, London
for Great Britain, Eire and the British Commonwealth (except Canada)

Le Chant du Monde, Paris
pour la France, Belgique, Luxembourg et les pays francophones de l'Afrique

Edition Fazer, Helsinki
for Finland

G. Ricordi & C. Milano
per l'Italia

Musikverlag Hans Sikorski, Hamburg
*für Deutschland, Dänemark, Island, Norwegen,
Schweden, Niederlande, Schweiz, Spanien, Portugal, Griechland, Türkei und Israel*

Univeral Edition A.G., Wien
für Österreich

Zen-On Music Company Ltd., Tokyo
for Japan

ISBN 978-0-7935-9770-3

G. SCHIRMER, Inc.

DISTRIBUTED BY

HAL•LEONARD®
CORPORATION
7777 W. BLUEMOUND RD. P.O. BOX 13819 MILWAUKEE, WI 53213

PETER AND THE WOLF

ENGLISH · FRENCH · SPANISH TEXT

Sergey Prokofiev, Op. 67
piano reduction by the composer

Andantino ♩ = 92

Early one morning Peter opened
the gate and went out into the big
green meadow.

*Un beau matin petit Pierre
ouvrit la porte du jardin et
sortit sur le pre.*

Una hermosa mañana Pedrito
abrió la puerta del jardín y salió
al campo para jugar.

On the branch of a big tree sat a
little bird, Peter's friend. "All is
quiet," chirped the bird gaily.

*Sur un grand arbre un petit oiseau,
ami de Pierre, était perché. "Tout
est tranquille ici," gozouilla-t-il
gaiement.*

En un arbol vió posado a un pajarito
amigo suyo que, cantando alegremente,
decía:"¡Oh, que tranquilidad reina aquí!"

2 Allegro ♩ = 176

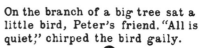

4

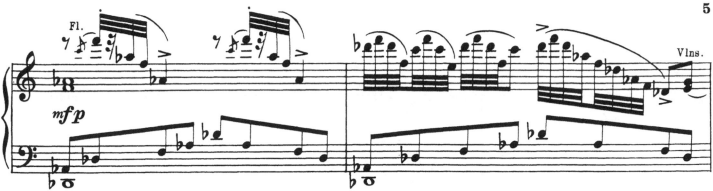

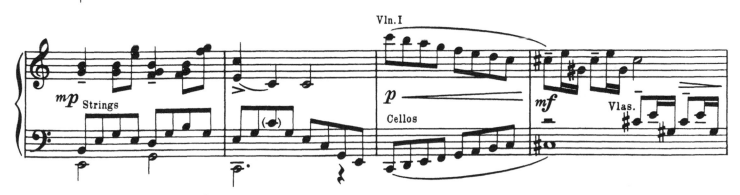

Soon a duck came waddling around. She was glad
that Peter had not closed the gate, and decided to
take a nice swim in the deep pond in the meadow.

*Un canard apparut derrière Pierre en se dandinant.
Il était bien content que Pierre n'eût pas fermé la
porte du jardin, et décida de plonger dans la mare
profonde du pré.*

Detrás de Pedrito caminaba con su andar
tambaleante un pato. Notando que el niño
dejaba la puerta abierta, el pato había salido también al campo, para ir a bañarse en
la laguna próxima.

6 L'istesso tempo ♩=♩

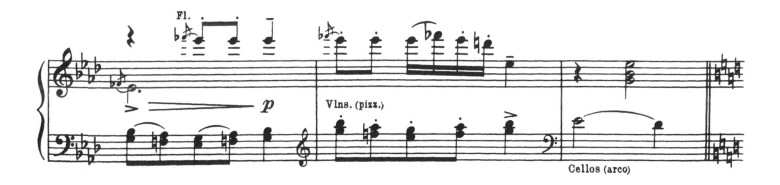

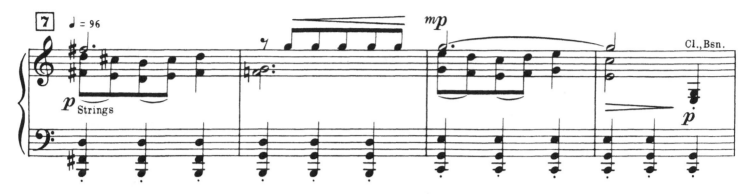

Seeing the duck, the little bird flew down upon the grass, settled next to the duck and shrugged his shoulders:

En voyant le canard, l'oiseau voltigea, se posa sur l'herbe à côté de lui et haussa les epaules:

Al ver al pato, el pajarito voló hacia él; se posó sobre la verde hierba cerca de la laguna, le miró encogiéndose de hombros le dijo:

"What kind of a bird are you, if you can't fly?" said he. To this the duck replied: "What kind of a bird are you, if you can't swim?" and dived into the pond.

"Quelle espèce d'oiseau es-tu, si tu ne sais pas voler!" dit-il. Sur quoi le canard lui répondit: "Quelle espèce d'oiseau es-tu, si tu ne sais pas nager!" et plongea dans la mare.

"¿Qué clase de pájaro eres tú, que no sabes volar?" A lo que el pato respondió: "¿Qué clase de pájaro eres tú, que no sabes nadar?" Y al decir esto zambulló en el agua.

8

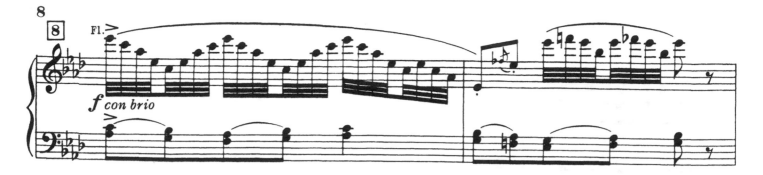

They argued and argued, the duck swimming in the pond, the little bird hopping along the shore.

Il discutèrent encore longtemps-le canard nageant dans la mare, l'oiseau voltigeant au bord.

Discutieron y discutieron, el pato nadando en la laguna y el pajarito saltando alredor por la orilla.

Suddenly, something caught Peter's attention. He noticed a cat crawling through the grass.

Soudain Pierre prèta l'oreille. Il remarqua qu'un chat rampait sur l'herbe.

De repente Pedrito vió algo que se arrastraba por entre la hierba, dirigiéndose hacia donde estaba el pajarito. ¡Era un gato!

The cat thought: "The bird is busy arguing, I'll just grab him."
Stealthily she crept toward him on her velvet paws.

*Le chat pensa: "Voici l'oiseau en discussion! Si j'en faisais mon
déjeuner?" Sans bruit, sur ses pattes de velours il s'en approcha.*

El gato pensaba: "Mientras el pajarito discute, yo llego y lo agarro."
Y seguía deslizándose silenciosamente con paso cauteloso.

"Look out!" shouted Peter, and the bird immediately flew up into the tree.

"Gare!" s'écria Pierre, et vite l'oiseau s'envola sur l'arbre,

"¡Cuidado, pajarito!" gritó el niño. Y, rápidamente, el pajarito voló hacia el árbol.

13 Allegro, ma non troppo ♩ = 152–160

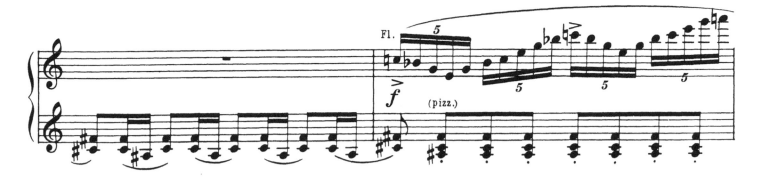

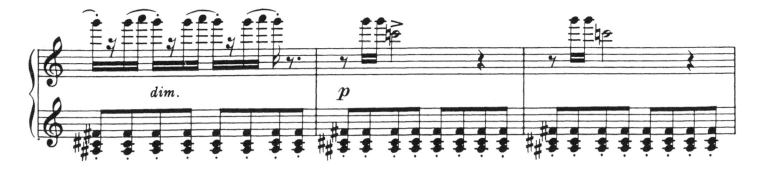

While the duck quacked angrily at the cat

Du milieu de la mare

Mientras tanto, desde enmedio de la laguna

12

from the middle of the pond.
le canard indigne fit coin coin au chat.
el pato le graznaba encolerizado al gato.

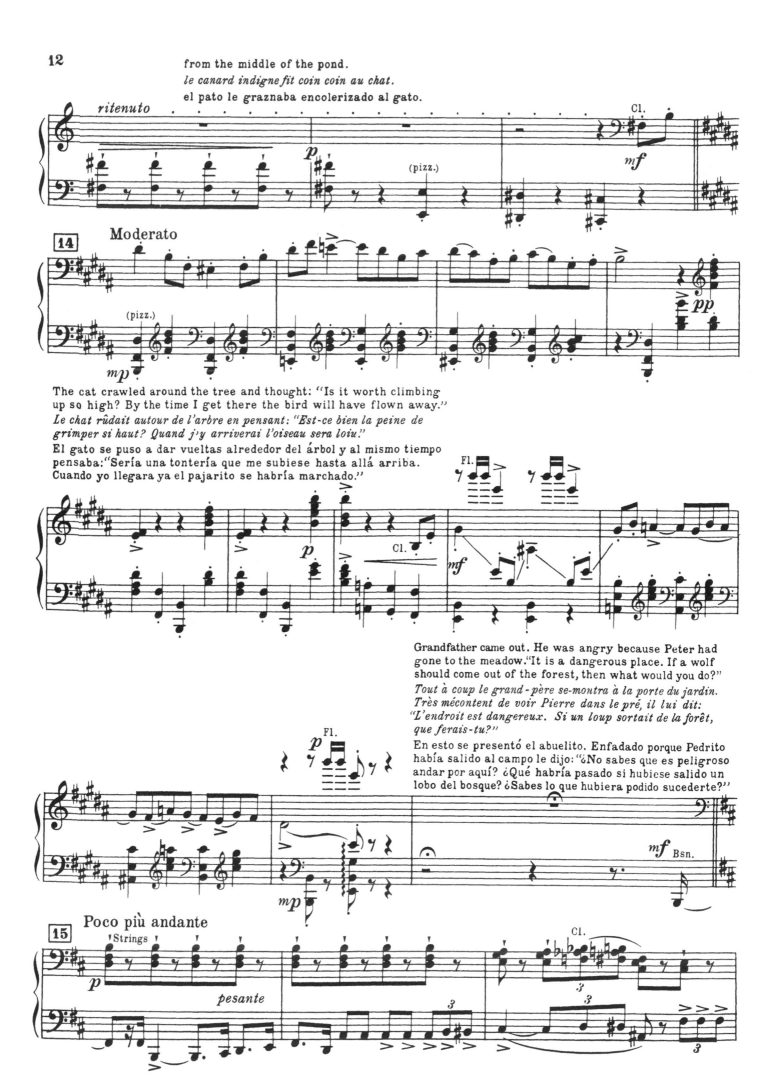

The cat crawled around the tree and thought: "Is it worth climbing up so high? By the time I get there the bird will have flown away."
Le chat rôdait autour de l'arbre en pensant: "Est-ce bien la peine de grimper si haut? Quand j'y arriverai l'oiseau sera loin."
El gato se puso a dar vueltas alrededor del árbol y al mismo tiempo pensaba:"Sería una tontería que me subiese hasta allá arriba. Cuando yo llegara ya el pajarito se habría marchado."

Grandfather came out. He was angry because Peter had gone to the meadow."It is a dangerous place. If a wolf should come out of the forest, then what would you do?"
Tout à coup le grand-père se-montra à la porte du jardin. Très mécontent de voir Pierre dans le pré, il lui dit: "L'endroit est dangereux. Si un loup sortait de la forêt, que ferais-tu?"
En esto se presentó el abuelito. Enfadado porque Pedrito había salido al campo le dijo: "¿No sabes que es peligroso andar por aquí? ¿Qué habría pasado si hubiese salido un lobo del bosque? ¿Sabes lo que hubiera podido sucederte?"

Peter paid no attention to his grandfather's words.
Boys like him are not afraid of wolves.

Pierre ne fit aucun cas des paroles du grand-père et déclara que des garçons comme lui n'ont pas peur des loups.

Entonces Pedrito contestó: "Los niños como yo no le tienen miedo a los lobos."

17 Andantino, come prima

Clar. & Vlns.

Fl.

But grandfather took Peter by the hand, led him home and locked the gate.

Mais le grand-père prit Pierre par la main, le conduisit à la maison et ferma la porte du jardin à clef.

18

El abuelito tomó a Pedrito de la mano y, después que ambos hubieron entrado en la casa, cerró la puerta cuidadosamente.

Andante

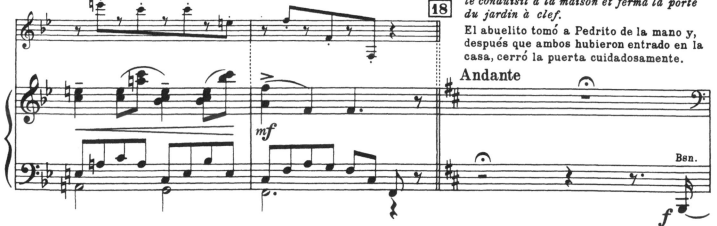

Bsn.

No sooner had Peter gone, than a big grey wolf came out of the forest.

Il était temps: Pierre était à peine rentré, qu'un gros loup gris apparut à la lisière de la forêt:

El abuelito tenía razón; pues no había hecho más que cerrar la puerta, cuando salió del bosque un gran lobo gris.

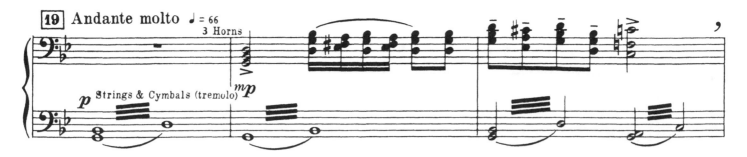

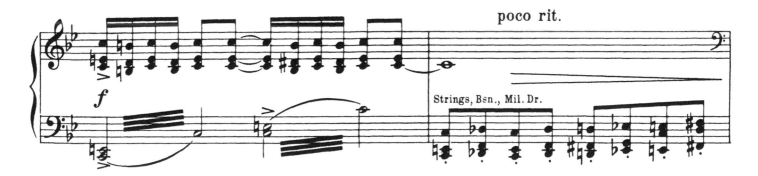

In a twinkling the cat climbed up the tree.
Le chat grimpa sur l'arbre en vitesse.
Como un relámpago, el gato se subió al árbol.

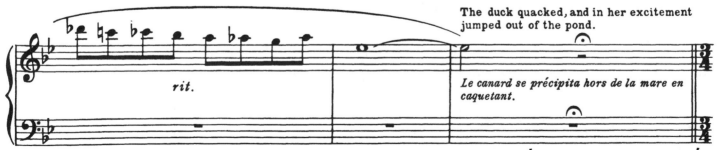

The duck quacked, and in her excitement jumped out of the pond.

Le canard se précipita hors de la mare en caquetant.

El pato saltó fuera de la laguna y comenzó a correr todo lo más aprisa que podía.

21 **Allegro** ♩ = 160

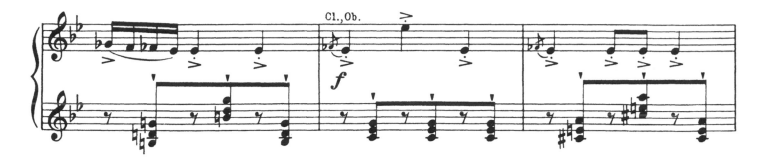

But no matter how hard the duck
tried to run...
Mais malgrè tous ses efforts...
Pero por muy aprisa que corriera
el pato...

she couldn't escape the wolf.
le loup courait plus vite.
más aprisa corria el lobo.

He was getting nearer...
Le voilà que s'approche...
Que ya se le iba acercando...

22

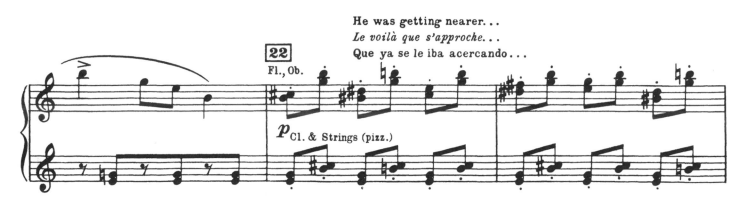

and nearer...
de plus en plus près...
y acercando...

catching up with her...
le voilà qui le rattrape...
hasta casi alcanzarle,

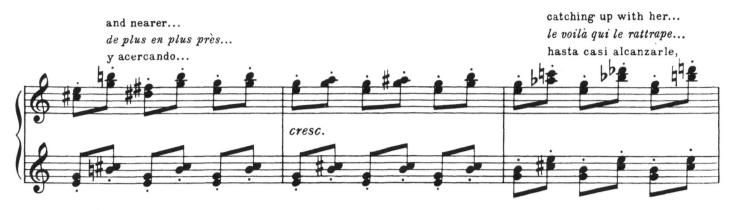

cresc.

ff Trpt. (muted)

and then he got her, and with one
gulp swallowed her.

ff

le saisit, et l'avala.

finalmente el lobo atrapó al pato y,
de un solo golpe, se lo tragó.

23 **Meno mosso**

Trpt.

Ob., Cl.

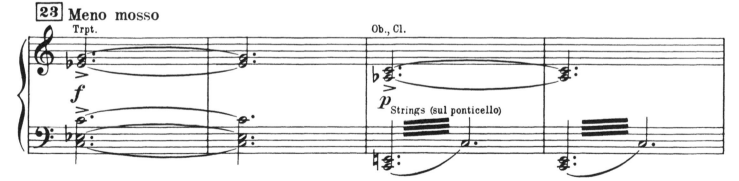

f

p Strings (sul ponticello)

Andante ♩ = 76

Cellos (flag.)

p doloroso

pp *doloroso ed espress.*

Ob.

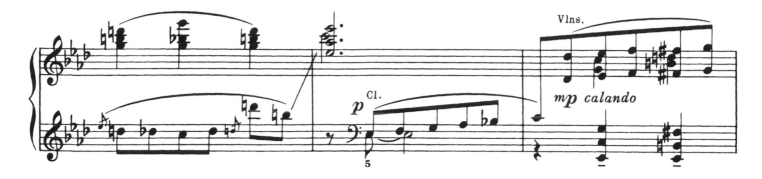

Vlns.

p Cl.

mp calando

And now, this is how things stood: the cat was sitting on one branch...

pp

Donc voici l'état des choses: le chat était assis sur une branche...

Veamos lo que sucedió entonces. El gato se había sentado en una rama del árbol...

25 **Allegretto** ♩ = 116

Cl.

p

Cellos & Bass (arco)

Fl.

p espr.

Strings

the bird on another...
l'oiseau sur une autre...
El pajarito se había posado en otra rama...

not too close to the cat.
à une bonne distance du chat.
pero todo lo más lejos posible del gato.

Bass (pizz.) & Bass Drum

Cl.

Cellos (arco)

Fl.

L.H.

Fl.

p espr.

Strings

Fl.

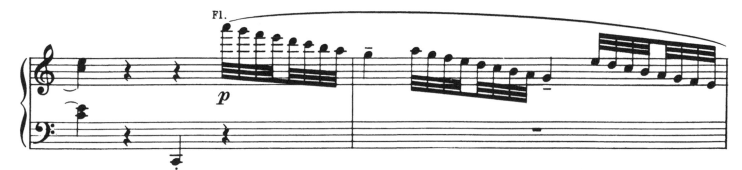

(pizz.)

While the wolf walked round and round the tree look-ing at them with greedy eyes.

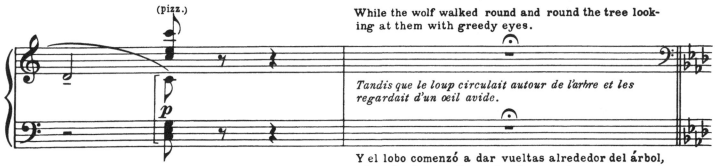

Tandis que le loup circulait autour de l'arbre et les regardait d'un œil avide.

Y el lobo comenzó a dar vueltas alrededor del árbol, mirando al **pajarito** y al gato con ojos voraces.

In the meantime, Peter, without the slightest fear, stood behind the closed gate watching all that was going on.

Pendant ce temps Pierre, debout près de la porte fermée, observait tout ce qui se passait sans aucune peur.

Pedrito, que observaba desde detrás de la puerta y veía todo lo que pasaba, pero que no tenía miedo en absoluto.

28 **Andantino, come prima** ♩ = 92

He ran home, got a strong rope and climbed up the high stone wall.
Il courut à la maison, prit une grosse corde et grimpa sur un haut mur.
Entró corriendo en la casa, tomó una cuerda fuerte, salió y se subió a lo alto de una tapia.

One of the branches of the tree around which the wolf was walking, stretched out over the wall.
Une des branches de l'arbre, autour duquel se promenait le loup, s'étendait jusqu'au mur.
Una de las ramas del árbol en que estaban el gato y el pajarito caía sobre esta tapia.

Grabbing hold of the branch,

Et en s'y cramponnant adroitement,

•Pedrito asió la rama

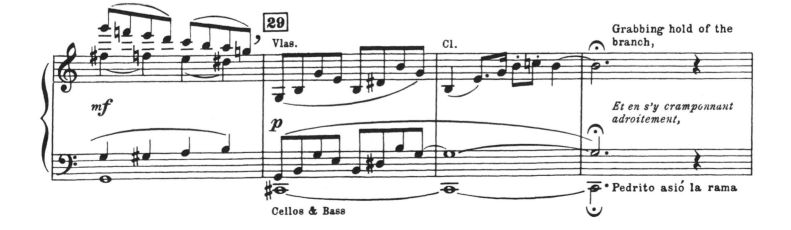

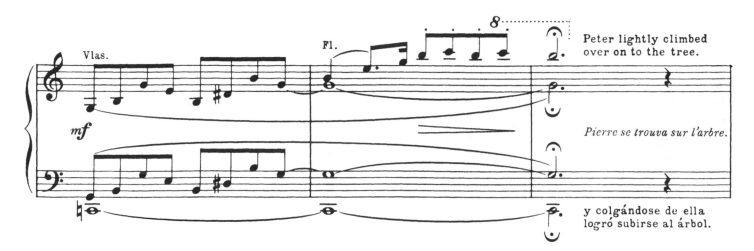

Peter lightly climbed
over on to the tree.

Pierre se trouva sur l'arbre.

y colgándose de ella
logró subirse al árbol.

Peter said to the bird: "Fly down and circle around
the wolf's head, only take care he doesn't catch you."

*Pierre dit à l'oiseau: „Va, voltige autour du museau du
loup, mais prends garde qu'il ne t'attrape.*

Ya en el árbol, Pedrito le dijo al pajarito: "Baja y
vuela alrededor del lobo para distraerlo; pero ten
cuidado no vaya a ser que te pille."

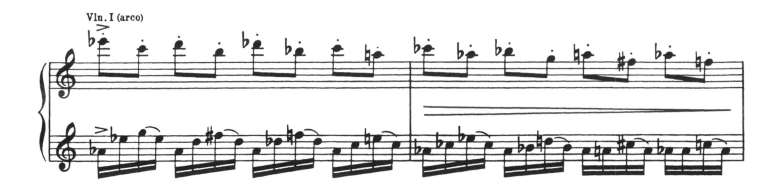

The bird almost touched the wolf's head with his wings while the wolf snapped angrily at him from this side and that.

31 Andante molto ♩ = 66

L'oiseau avec ses ailes touchait presque le gueule de l'animal, qui, furieux, sautait de tous côtés pour l'attraper.

El pajarito comenzó a volar tan cerca del lobo, que casi le rozaba la nariz con las alas; y el lobo, lleno de ira, trataba en vano de alcanzarlo dando tarascadas acá y allá.

26

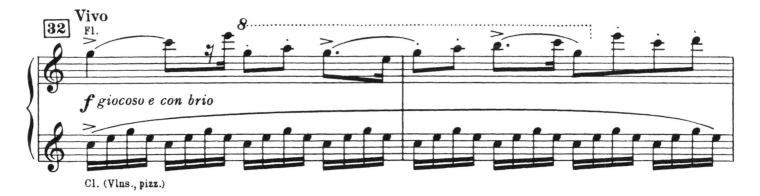

How the bird did worry the wolf! How he wanted to catch him! But the
bird was too clever, and the wolf simply couldn't do anything about it.

*Oh que l'oiseau agaçait le loup! Comme il voulait l'attraper! Mais l'oiseau
était bien trop adroit pour se laisser prendre.*

El lobo estaba enfurecido. ¡Como le hubiera gustado comerse el pajarito!
Pero éste era demasiado rápido y el lobo no podía hacerle nada.

33 **Andante**

Meanwhile Peter made a lasso and carefully letting it down,

34 **Allegro** ♩ = 160

*Durant ce manège, Pierre fit un noeud coulant à la
corde et le descendit avec beaucoup de précautions.*

pp Vln. I (muted)

Mientras el lobo acechaba al pajarito, Pedrito hizo con
la cuerda un lazo como el de los vaqueros y se lo arrojó.

Vln. I sul G

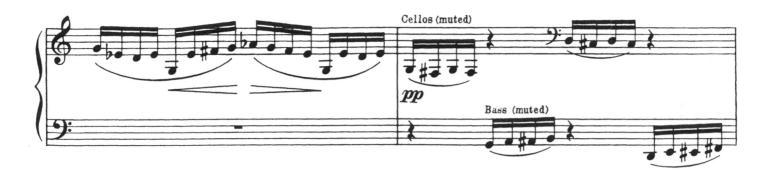

caught the wolf by the tail and
pulled with all his might.

35 **Poco meno mosso** ♩ = 138

*le passa à la queue du loup te tira
de toutes ses forces.*

ff *marcato e furioso*

Hrns.

El lazo le cayó encima y lo agar-
ró por la cola. Entonces Pedrito
haló con todas sus fuerzas.

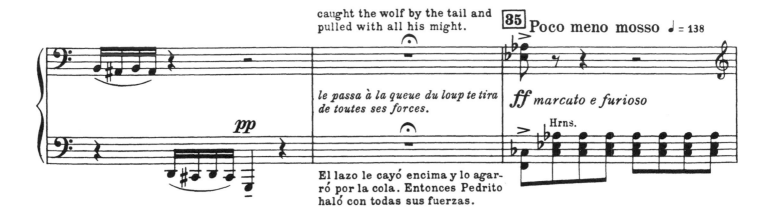

Trpt. & Strgs.

Trpt. & Strgs.

sf

ff

marcato

f

Feeling himself caught, the wolf began to
jump wildly trying to get loose.

Moderato (Meno mosso)

Trpt. (muted) & Vln. I (sul pont.)

*Le loup, sentant qu'il était pris, pleind de rage
se mit à sauter, essayant de se libérer.*

f *marcato*

Trb. & Cello, Bass (pizz.)

El lobo, al verse sujeto, comenzó a saltar
violentamente tratando de soltarse.

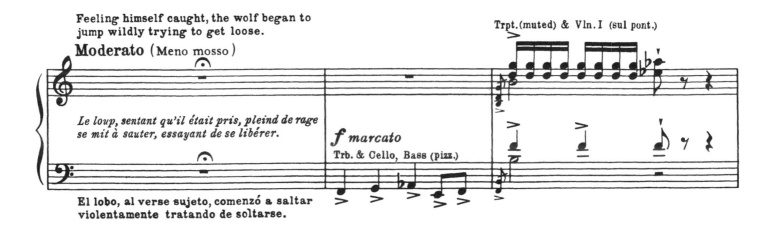

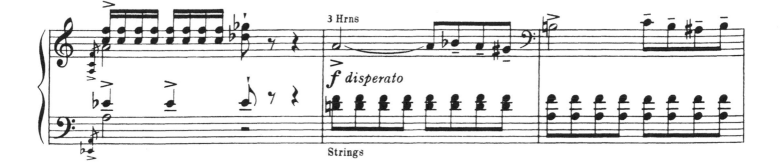

But Peter tied the other end of the rope to the tree,
Mais Pierre attacha l'autre bout de la corde à l'arbre.
Pedrito amarró al árbol el otro extremo de la cuerda.

and the wolf's jumping only made the rope around his tail tighter.

Les sauts du loup ne faisaient que resserrer le nœud coulant.

Y mientras más halaba el lobo, mas se apretaba el nudo que le tenía atado.

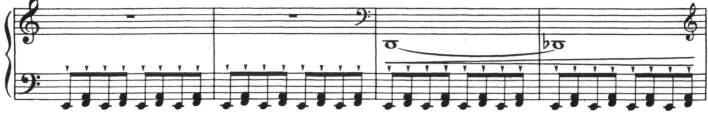

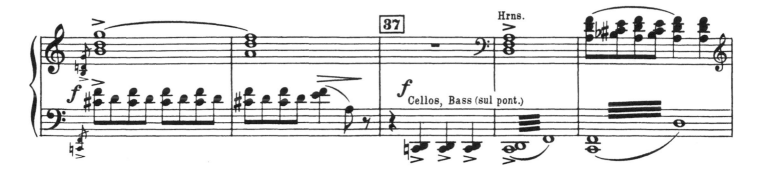

Just then...

A ce moment...

En aquel momento...

the hunters came out of the woods,

des chasseurs apparurent à la lisière de la forêt.

salieron del bosque unos cazadores.

following the wolf's trail and shooting as they came.

Ils suivaient les traces du loup et tiraient des coups de fusils.

Estos cazadores venían per-siguiendo al lobo y continua-ron haciéndole fuego con sus escopetas.

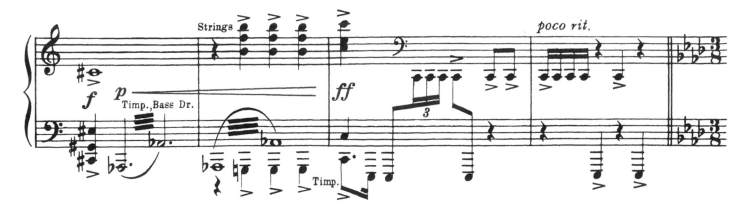

But Peter sitting in the tree, said: "Don't shoot!
The bird and I have already caught the wolf. Now
help us take him to the zoo."

41 Andante ♩. = 63

*Pierre leur cria du haut de l'arbre: „Cela ne vaut
pas la peine de tirer! Nous avons déjà attrapé le
loup, l'oiseau et moi! Aidez-nous a l'emmener au
jardin zoologique."*

Entonces Pedrito les gritó desde el árbol:"¡No
le disparen más, que ya lo hemos atrapado entre
el pajarito y yo! ¡Vengan y ayúdennos a llevarlo
al Jardín Zoológico!"

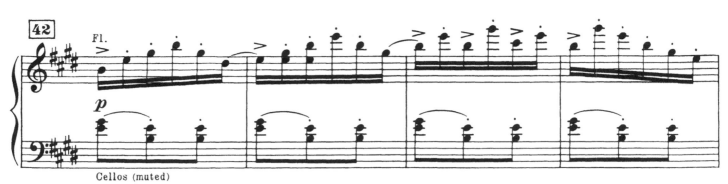

Fl.

p

Cellos (muted)

Bsn.

mp

+Cl.

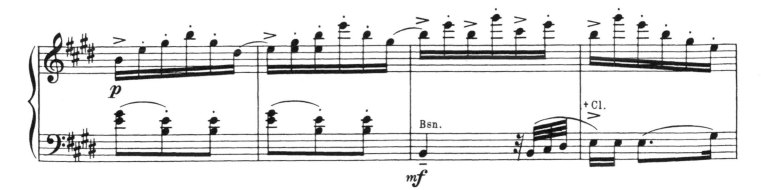

p

Bsn.

mf

+Cl.

mp

43 And now...
Moderato ♩ = 104

Hrns.

Vlns.

1

Imagine the triumphant
procession:

Et voila...

p

*Figurez vous le marche
triomphale:*

Y ahora...

¡imaginense aquella mar-
cha triumfal!

Peter at the head;
Pierre marchait en tête,
Primero iba Pedrito.

44 Hrns.

after him the hunters leading the wolf;
les chasseurs conduisaient le loup.
Despúes seguían los cazadorez arrastrando al lobo.

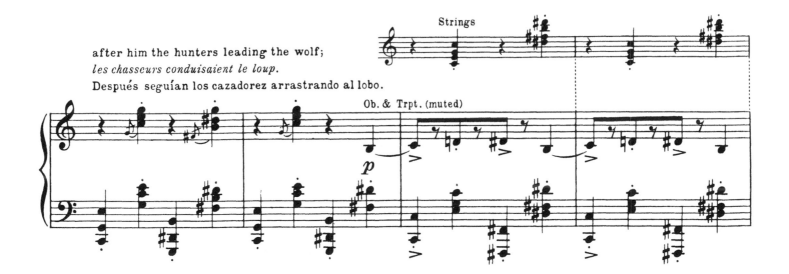

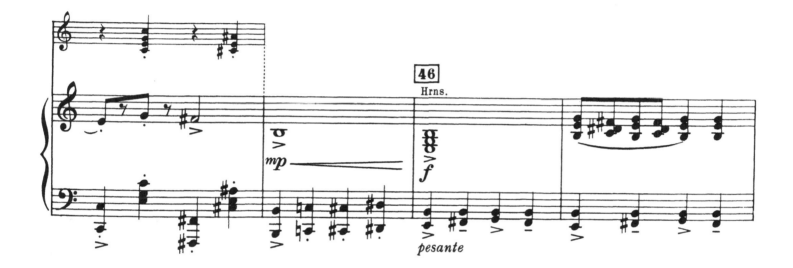

47 Poco più mosso (Allegro moderato) ♩ = 116

and winding up the procession, grandfather and the cat. Grandfather tossed his head discontentedly: "Well, and if Peter hadn't caught the wolf? What then?"

Le grand-père avec le chat marchaient en queue. Le grand-père, mécontent, hochait la tête en disant: "Eh bien, et si Pierre n'avait pas attrapé le loup? Quoi alors?"

Y finalmente el abuelito llevando al gato. Por cierto que, al caminar, agitaba la cabeza y, como hablando consigo mismo, repetía: "¿Qué habría pasado si Pedrito no hubiese agarrado al lobo? ¿Qué hubiera sucedido entonces?"

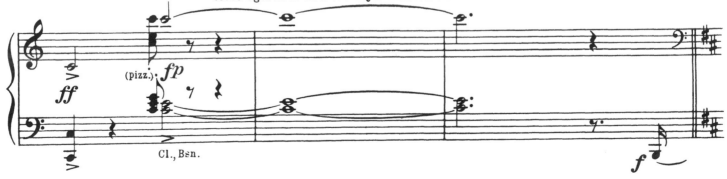

49 L'istesso tempo

50

Above them flew the bird chirping merrily: "My, what brave
fellows we are, Peter and I! Look what we have caught!"

L'oiseau voltigeait au dessus en gazouillant gaiement:"Voilà
sommes, Pierre et moi! Voilà qui nous avons attrapé!"

Mientras tanto el pajarito, revoloteando en torno de ellos,
piaba alegremente diciéndoles una y otra vez: "¡Vean lo
valientes que somos Pedrito y yo! ¡Miren, miren lo que
hemos cazado! ¡¡¡Un lobo!!!

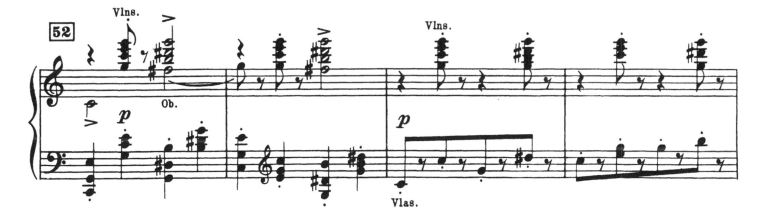

And if you would listen very carefully, you could hear the duck quacking inside the wolf; because the wolf in his haste had swallowed her alive.

Et si vous écoutiez attentivement, vous entendriez comme le canard gémit dans le ventre du loup; le loup dans sa hâte l'avait avalé tout entier et le canard était resté vivant.

Y si hubieran escuchado atentamente, habrían oido graznar al pato en la paza del lobo; pues éste, en su precipitación, ¡se lo había tragado vivo!

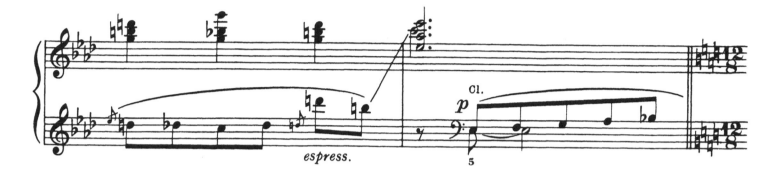

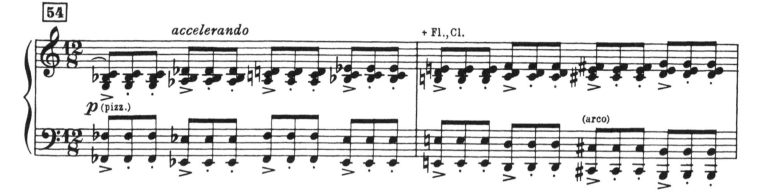